Lifesize
Rainforest

Written by Anita Ganeri
Illustrated by
Stuart Jackson-Carter

KINGFISHER

KINGFISHER

First published 2014 by Kingfisher
an imprint of Macmillan Children's Books
20 New Wharf Road, London N1 9RR
Associated companies throughout the world
www.panmacmillan.com

Consultant: Michael Bright
Editor: Clare Hibbert
In-house editor: Carly Madden
Design and styling: Maj Jackson-Carter
Cover design: Mike Davis

ISBN 978-0-7534-3635-6

3 5 7 9 8 6 4 2

2TR/1015/WKT/UG/128MA

A CIP catalogue record for this book is available from the British Library.

Printed in China

Contents

How many female frogs can you spot? Turn to page 32 to check.

Blue poison dart frogs

As a male poison dart frog sits and calls, a group of females gathers. Two of them even start to fight! Just one will become his mate. After mating, both parents guard the eggs until they hatch. Then they carry the tadpoles to tiny, tree-top ponds, formed from water caught in bromeliad flowers.

Bee hummingbirds

A pair of the world's tiniest birds flits around a hummingbird bush. Using their long, pointed bills, they reach deep inside the scarlet flowers to drink the sweet nectar. To feed, bee hummingbirds hover in one place and beat their wings in a figure-of-eight pattern 80 times a second – so fast that they look like a blur.

Goliath beetles

Handsome Goliath beetles do battle on a tree branch.
These two are males, fighting over territory or to win a
female's attention. Gripping on tightly with their sharp
claws, the beetles push at each other with their Y-shaped
horns, until the unlucky loser tumbles off the tree.

Philippine tarsiers

In the rainforest, night is falling. A baby Philippine tarsier clings to its mother's back as she hunts for insects to eat. After locating her prey with her enormous eyes, she will catch it in her hands. Her long, slender fingers form a cage to stop the flapping insect from getting away.

Queen Alexandra's birdwing butterflies

A pair of Queen Alexandra's birdwing butterflies flies high above the rainforest canopy. It is easy to tell male and female apart – the male is smaller and more colourful. The biggest butterflies in the world, these magnificent insects began life as tiny eggs laid on poisonous pipevine leaves.

Raggiana bird of paradise

During the breeding season, a male Raggiana bird of paradise puts on a spectacular show. He takes up his perch on the branch of a tree. Then he lowers his head, claps his wings, shrieks loudly and puffs out his gorgeous tail feathers. This display is aimed at attracting a female – she chooses the showiest male.

Parson's chameleon

Standing perfectly still on a tree branch, a Parson's chameleon grips tightly with its mitten-like feet. Only its big, bulging eyes show any signs of movement, swivelling round in search of insects. When the chameleon spots one, it shoots out its long, sticky tongue, and snaps up the prey, lightning fast.

Golden-crowned flying fox

A golden-crowned flying fox, one of the world's biggest bats, spends the day roosting upside-down on a branch. It shares its tree with other flying foxes for protection from enemies. When night falls, the bat flies many kilometres through the forest searching for juicy figs – its favourite food.

Mandrill

With a face of red and blue and a bright bottom to match, a male mandrill is a magnificent sight. Striking markings attract females but also make it easier for the monkeys to follow each other through the thick forest. Mandrills live in large family groups called troops – the male with the boldest colours becomes troop leader.

Jaguar

As evening falls in the rainforest, a solitary jaguar sets out to hunt for food. This beautiful beast has a powerful, muscular body and jaws strong enough to bite through a turtle's shell. A superb swimmer and climber, the jaguar lies in wait for prey, then leaps out when a victim comes near.

Malayan tapir

Shuffling slowly through the undergrowth, a Malayan tapir makes frequent stops to munch on twigs, leaves and fruit. It guides the food into its mouth with its long, fleshy snout. The tapir is mostly out and about at night-time, using the same well-worn paths through the forest to find the best places to feed.

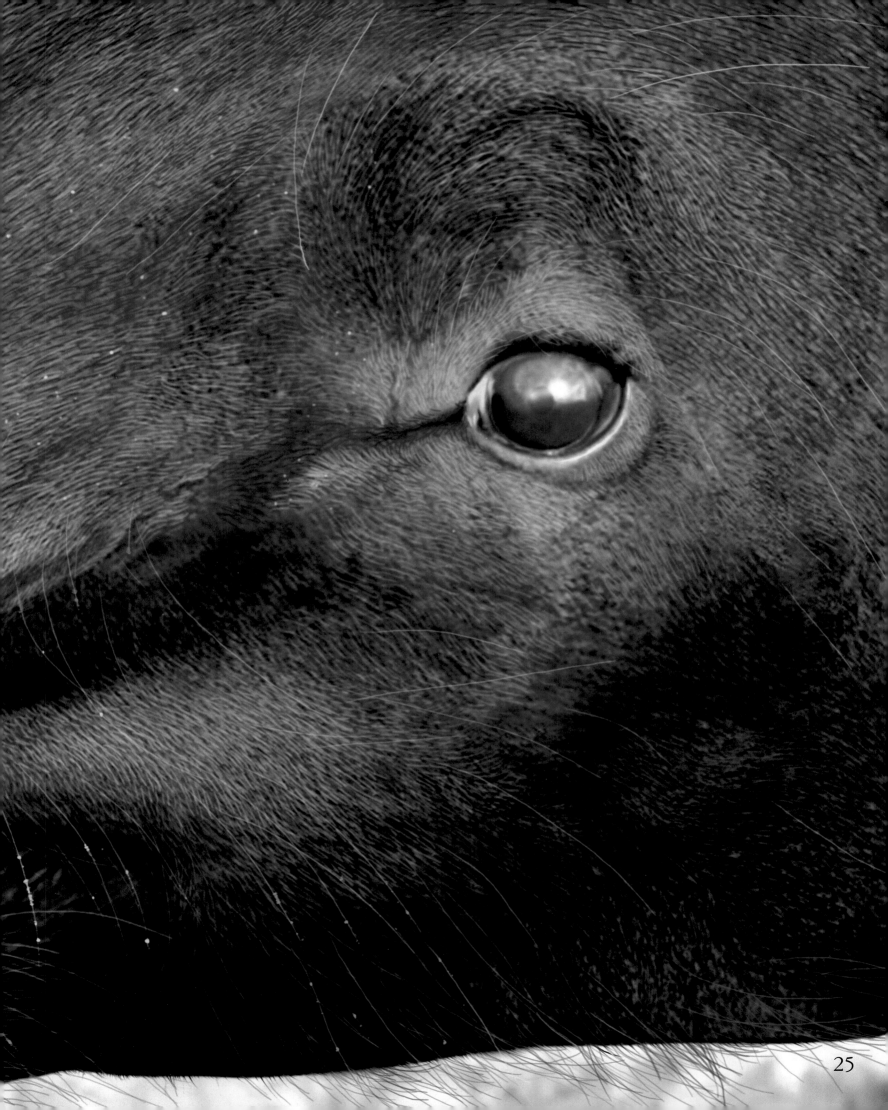

Green anaconda

A green anaconda lurks in the river. Having eyes and nostrils on top of its head means it can still see and breathe. The snake waits for a tapir or other animal to come down to the water's edge, grabs it, coils around it and squeezes it to death. Then the anaconda swallows its meal whole.

Animal facts

Each frog has its own unique pattern of black spots.

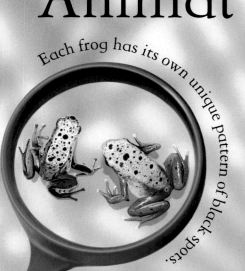

Blue poison dart frog

Rainforest habitat: Suriname and Brazil, South America

Length: 3–4.5cm

Weight: Around 8g

Diet: Mostly insects

Average lifespan: 4–6 years

Amazing fact: The blue poison dart frog's eye-catching colours are not simply for show. They warn other animals that the frog is deadly poisonous to eat.

UNDER THREAT

Bee hummingbirds lay eggs the size of peas in tiny, cup-shaped nests.

Bee hummingbird

UNDER THREAT

Rainforest habitat: Cuba, Central America

Length: Around 5.5cm

Weight: Up to 1.9g

Diet: Nectar and small insects

Average lifespan: Up to 7 years

Amazing fact: To keep up their energy, bee hummingbirds have to eat half their weight in food each day and drink up to eight times their weight in water.

These butterflies sip flower nectar using their long, straw-like tongues.

UNDER THREAT

Queen Alexandra's birdwing butterfly

Rainforest habitat: Papua New Guinea, Oceania

Length: 8cm (female); 6cm (male)

Wingspan: 30cm (female); 19cm (male)

Weight: Around 12g (female); around 9g (male)

Diet: Nectar

Average lifespan: 3 months (adult)

Amazing fact: Queen Alexandra's birdwing butterfly was discovered in 1906. It was named as a compliment to the British queen at that time, Alexandra, wife of King Edward VII.

Females lay their eggs in the soil. They dig holes with their heads.

Tarsiers have pads on their fingers and toes to help them to grip.

Goliath beetle

Rainforest habitat: Africa

Length: Up to 11cm (male); up to 8cm (female)

Weight: Around 50g

Diet: Tree sap and fruit

Average lifespan: Less than 1 year

Amazing fact: Goliath beetles are some of the biggest insects in the world. Male beetles can grow as big as your hand and weigh as much as three mice.

Philippine tarsier

Rainforest habitat: Philippines, Southeast Asia

Length of head and body: Up to 16cm

Length of tail: Up to 27.5cm

Weight: Up to 165g

Diet: Mostly insects, especially crickets and grasshoppers

Average lifespan: 10 years (in captivity)

Amazing fact: A Philippine tarsier cannot swivel its eyes in their sockets but can turn its head almost all the way round to look out for prey.

UNDER THREAT

UNDER THREAT

Animals are under threat if their numbers are falling and they risk becoming extinct (dying out forever). Or they may be under threat because their habitat is disappearing.

A chameleon's tongue is more than twice as long as its body.

Birds of paradise are related to crows and starlings.

Parson's chameleon

Rainforest habitat: Madagascar

Length: Up to 70cm

Weight: Around 700g

Diet: Insects, lizards and birds

Average lifespan: More than 6 years

Amazing fact: A Parson's chameleon can change the colour of its skin to blend in with its surroundings, communicate with other chameleons or regulate its body temperature.

Raggiana bird of paradise

Rainforest habitat: Papua New Guinea, Oceania

Length: Around 34cm

Wingspan: Up to 63cm

Weight: Around 270g (male); around 175g (female)

Diet: Fruit, berries and insects

Average lifespan: Unknown, but other birds of paradise live more than 30 years in captivity

Amazing fact: Groups of up to ten Raggiana birds of paradise gather in one tree. The same tree may have been used by many generations of birds.

The golden-crowned flying fox gets its name from its crown of golden hairs.

UNDER THREAT

Golden-crowned flying fox

Rainforest habitat: Philippines, Southeast Asia

Length: Up to 31cm

Wingspan: Up to 1.7m

Weight: Around 1.2kg

Diet: Fruit, mostly figs

Average lifespan: 15 years

Amazing fact: A young flying fox will cling to its mother's fur with its claws. She fans it with one of her wings to keep it cool.

Mandrill

Rainforest habitat: West Africa

Length: Up to 90cm

Weight: Up to 35kg

Diet: Fruit (50%); seeds, leaves and flowers (45%); insects, spiders, amphibians, eggs, birds and small mammals (5%)

Average lifespan: 20 years

Amazing fact: Mandrills have huge canine teeth, more than 5cm long. They look scary when they shake their heads and bare their teeth but actually, they are being friendly.

UNDER THREAT

Mandrills store food in large pouches in their cheeks for eating later.

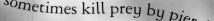

Jaguar

Rainforest habitat: Central, South and southwestern North America

Length of head and body: Up to 1.85m

Length of tail: Up to 91cm

Weight: Up to 113kg

Diet: Mammals, reptiles and fish

Average lifespan: 12–15 years

Amazing fact: Most jaguars have tawny-orange fur with black rosette-shaped markings. But some have such dark coats that you can hardly see their spots.

Jaguars sometimes kill prey by piercing the skull with their sharp teeth and biting into the brain.

UNDER THREAT

Tapirs cannot see very well but have sharp senses of hearing and smell.

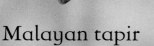

Malayan tapir

Rainforest habitat: Southeast Asia

Length: Up to 2.4m

Weight: Up to 540kg

Diet: Twigs, leaves and fruit

Average lifespan: Up to 30 years

Amazing fact: A young tapir has spots and stripes that blend in with the dappled forest light, hiding it from harm. The adult's striking blocks of black and white also act as a disguise, making the tapir look more like a rock than an animal!

Green anaconda

Rainforest habitat: South America and Trinidad

Length: Up to 6m

Weight: More than 100kg

Diet: Mammals, reptiles, fish and birds

Average lifespan: 10 years

Amazing fact: Green anacondas have such stretchy jaws that they can swallow prey whole, even if it is many times bigger than their heads.

A group of green anacondas is called a bed or knot.

Saving rainforest animals

Every day, vast patches of rainforest are cut down for timber, and to make space for farms, mines and new roads. This leaves rainforest animals with nowhere to live or find food. Scientists, governments and conservation groups are working hard to try to find ways of saving the rainforests. One idea is to set aside protected areas where logging and mining are banned. This is already happening in parts of Central America.

Why are jaguars in danger?

Their rainforest home is being destroyed.

They are killed for preying on farmers' cattle.

They are hunted for their beautiful fur.

Five groups working to save rainforest animals:

The Amazon Conservation Association tries to protect the wildlife of the Amazon rainforest in Peru and Bolivia by working with local people and companies. www.amazonconservation.org

The Orangutan Project runs conservation projects and rescue centres for orang-utans that are losing their rainforest home to make way for palm oil plantations. www.orangutan.org.au

The Rainforest Alliance works to safeguard the world's rainforests by finding ways in which people, plants and animals can all exist together. www.rainforest-alliance.org

The Rainforest Foundation helps local rainforest people around the world to keep their homes and to save the forest and its wildlife for the future. www.rainforestfoundationuk.org

The WWF works to preserve the world's wild places and their wildlife. Its site has details about how to sponsor a piece of rainforest or adopt a rainforest animal. www.wwf.org.uk

Answer: There are eight females in the picture on pages 4 and 5 – the ninth frog is the male!